KNOW YOUR FOOD

WATER

KNOW YOUR FOOD

Fats and Cholesterol

Fiber

Flavorings, Colorings, and Preservatives

Food Safety

Genetically Modified Foods

Gluten

Organic Foods

Protein

Salt

Starch and Other Carbohydrates

Sugar and Sweeteners

Vitamins and Minerals

Water

Water

MICHAEL CENTORE

Mason Crest
450 Parkway Drive, Suite D
Broomall, PA 19008
www.masoncrest.com

MTM Publishing, Inc.
435 West 23rd Street, #8C
New York, NY 10011
www.mtmpublishing.com

President: Valerie Tomaselli
Vice President, Book Development: Hilary Poole
Designer: Annemarie Redmond
Copyeditor: Peter Jaskowiak
Editorial Assistant: Leigh Eron

Series ISBN: 978-1-4222-3733-5
Hardback ISBN: 978-1-4222-3746-5
E-Book ISBN: 978-1-4222-8053-9

Library of Congress Cataloging-in-Publication Data
Names: Centore, Michael, 1980- author.
Title: Water / by Michael Centore.
Description: Broomall, PA: Mason Crest, [2018] | Series: Know your food |
    Audience: Age 12+ | Audience: Grade 7 to 8. | Includes index.
Identifiers: LCCN 2017000436 (print) | LCCN 2017009540 (ebook) | ISBN
    9781422237465 (hardback: alk. paper) | ISBN 9781422280539 (ebook)
Subjects: LCSH: Water—Physiological effect—Juvenile literature. |
    Dehydration (Physiology)—Juvenile literature.
Classification: LCC QP535.H1 C46 2018 (print) | LCC QP535.H1 (ebook) | DDC
    612/.01522—dc23
LC record available at https://lccn.loc.gov/2017000436

Printed and bound in the United States of America.

First printing
9 8 7 6 5 4 3 2 1

TABLE OF CONTENTS

Key Icons to Look for:

 Words to Understand: These words with their easy-to-understand definitions will increase the reader's understanding of the text, while building vocabulary skills.

 Sidebars: This boxed material within the main text allows readers to build knowledge, gain insights, explore possibilities, and broaden their perspectives by weaving together additional information to provide realistic and holistic perspectives.

 Educational Videos: Readers can view videos by scanning our QR codes, which will provide them with additional educational content to supplement the text. Examples include news coverage, moments in history, speeches, iconic sports moments, and much more.

 Text-Dependent Questions: These questions send the reader back to the text for more careful attention to the evidence presented there.

 Research Projects: Readers are pointed toward areas of further inquiry connected to each chapter. Suggestions are provided for projects that encourage deeper research and analysis.

 Series Glossary of Key Terms: This back-of-the-book glossary contains terminology used throughout the series. Words found here increase the reader's ability to read and comprehend higher-level books and articles in this field.

SERIES INTRODUCTION

In the early 19th century, a book was published in France called *Physiologie du goût* (*The Physiology of Taste*), and since that time, it has never gone out of print. Its author was Jean Anthelme Brillat-Savarin. Brillat-Savarin is still considered to be one of the great food writers, and he was, to use our current lingo, arguably the first "foodie." Among other pearls, *Physiologie du goût* gave us one of the quintessential aphorisms about dining: "Tell me what you eat, and I will tell you what you are."

This concept was introduced to Americans in the 20th century by a nutritionist named Victor Lindlahr, who wrote simply, "You are what you eat." Lindlahr interpreted the saying literally: if you eat healthy food, he argued, you will become a healthy person.

But Brillat-Savarin likely had something a bit more metaphorical in mind. His work suggested that the dishes we create and consume have not only nutritional implications, but ethical, philosophical, and even political implications, too.

To be clear, Brillat-Savarin had a great deal to say on the importance of nutrition. In his writings he advised people to limit their intake of "floury and starchy substances," and for that reason he is sometimes considered to be the inventor of the low-carb diet. But Brillat-Savarin also took the idea of dining extremely seriously. He was devoted to the notion of pleasure in eating and was a fierce advocate of the importance of being a good host. In fact, he went so far as to say that anyone who doesn't make an effort to feed his guests "does not deserve to have friends." Brillat-Savarin also understood that food was at once deeply personal and extremely social. "Cooking is one of the oldest arts," he wrote, "and one that has rendered us the most important service in civic life."

Modern diners and cooks still grapple with the many implications of Brillat-Savarin's most famous statement. Certainly on a nutritional level, we understand that a diet that's low in fat and high in whole grains is a key to healthy living. This is no minor issue. Unless our current course is reversed, today's "obesity epidemic" is poised to significantly reduce the life spans of future generations.

Meanwhile, we are becoming increasingly aware of how the decisions we make at supermarkets can ripple outward, impacting our neighborhoods, nations, and the earth as a whole. Increasing numbers of us are demanding organically produced foods and ethically sourced ingredients. Some shoppers reject products that contain artificial ingredients like trans fats or high-fructose corn syrup. Some adopt gluten-free or vegan diets, while others "go Paleo" in the hopes of returning to a more "natural" way of eating. A simple trip to the supermarket can begin to feel like a personality test—the implicit question is not only "what does a *healthy* person eat?," but also "what does a *good* person eat?"

The Know Your Food series introduces students to these complex issues by looking at the various components that make up our meals: carbohydrates, fats, proteins, vitamins, and so on. Each volume focuses on one component and explains its function in our bodies, how it gets into food, how it changes when cooked, and what happens when we consume too much or too little. The volumes also look at food production—for example, how did the food dye called Red No. 2 end up in our food, and why was it taken out? What are genetically modified organisms, and are they safe or not? Along the way, the volumes also explore different diets, such as low-carb, low-fat, vegetarian, and gluten-free, going beyond the hype to examine their potential benefits and possible downsides.

Each chapter features definitions of key terms for that specific section, while a Series Glossary at the back provides an overview of words that are most important to the set overall. Chapters have Text-Dependent Questions at the end, to help students assess their comprehension of the most important material, as well as suggested Research Projects that will help them continue their exploration. Last but not least, QR codes accompany each chapter; students with cell phones or tablets can scan these codes for videos that will help bring the topics to life. (Those without devices can access the videos via an Internet browser; the addresses are included at the end of the Further Reading list.)

In the spirit of Brillat-Savarin, the volumes in this set look beyond nutrition to also consider various historical, political, and ethical aspects of food. Whether it's the key role that sugar played in the slave trade, the implications of industrial meat production in the fight against climate change, or the short-sighted political decisions that resulted in the water catastrophe in Flint, Michigan, the Know Your Food series introduces students to the ways in which a meal can be, in a real sense, much more than just a meal.

THE BASIS OF LIFE

 ## WORDS TO UNDERSTAND

aquatic: relating to things located in or near water.

electrolyte: a mineral in the body that is able to conduct an electric charge.

hydration: the act of combining a substance with water; to add water to the body.

hydrologic cycle: the continual circulation of water between land or water surfaces on Earth and the atmosphere.

lubricate: to make something move smoothly.

metabolites: the products of chemical reactions that occur within living organisms.

perspire: to release sweat through the pores of the skin, due to heat, physical activity, or other stresses.

solvent: something that can dissolve other substances.

It covers 70 percent of the planet and makes up over half of your body weight. In one way or another, it is vital to the health and sustenance of all life on Earth. Plants need it to produce oxygen, fish and other ocean animals rely on it for their habitat, and humans need it to grow food. Without it, the cells of living organisms could not take in nutrients or shuttle out toxins. It's so crucial, in fact, that when scientists are looking for life on other planets, they check to see if it's there first. The name of this incredible substance? Water.

FOOD AND WATER

Food and water are inextricably connected. It's not only that we need both to survive, but also that water itself is a necessary ingredient in the growth and production of so much of what we eat. Take beef, for instance. Between growing the grass, corn, wheat, and other grains used to feed a cow, plus what it drinks, plus what the farm needs for cleaning and processing, it can take over 1,800 gallons (6813.7 liters) of water to produce a single pound of beef. We may not see that water when we sit down to eat, but it's there regardless. It even has a name: the British geographer Tony Allan has coined the term "virtual water" to describe the many gallons "hidden" in our food.

Beyond production, we need water for food preparation. The kitchen of an average restaurant goes through about 2,900 gallons (almost 11,000 liters) each day, which are used for cooking and cleaning up after meals. While we use much less in

When you add up the water cows drink, the water needed to grow their food, and the water to process and clean the meat, an average hamburger requires a stunning amount of water to get to your plate.

A lot of water used by restaurants isn't even seen by diners.

VIRTUAL WATER

 Other examples of virtual water include the 11 gallons (41.6 liters) it takes to make a single slice of bread and the 53 gallons (200.6 liters) for an egg. To think about it another way, it takes approximately 1 liter of water to produce every calorie we eat.

This single slice of toast and one egg required about 64 gallons (242.2 liters) of water to create.

our own homes—about 400 gallons (1,514 liters) total each day, with over 15 percent funneled through kitchen and bathroom faucets—the principle is still the same: water is not only for staying hydrated, but also for keeping ourselves fed. Consider the many common cooking methods that require water:

- **Boiling.** This involves heating water to the point where it begins to turn from a liquid to a gas, at 212°F (100°C). Vegetables, pasta, rice, and even meats can all be cooked by immersion in boiling water. A low boil is called a *simmer.*

- **Steaming.** Here, food is placed in a basket or other container above boiling water. The warm vapor of the water cooks the food. Vegetables are often steamed, since the method preserves more of the vitamins and minerals than intensive boiling.

- **Blanching.** Blanched food is dropped into boiling water for a brief period, removed, and then dunked in ice-cold water to stop it from cooking. Blanching can remove unpleasant flavors or bitterness from foods, and it can preserve the color of vegetables prior to freezing them.

- *Sous-vide.* French for "under vacuum," this is a more involved method, where food is sealed in plastic bags and then placed in a temperature-controlled water bath. The technique cooks the food more evenly and helps retain moisture and nutrients.

- *Bain-marie.* Another French term, this literally means "bath of Mary," perhaps for the gentle way it cooks things. In a *bain-marie*, a smaller container holding food is fitted above a larger container holding boiling water. The heat from the water cooks the food. The *bain-marie* method is often used to melt chocolate so it doesn't burn.

Whether we're getting takeout or eating in, tending our own vegetable garden, or buying produce from the supermarket, buckets of water lie behind our every food decision. To be aware of the link between water and food can help us understand water's central place in our lives, and why, in an age of drought, it is so important to monitor our usage.

PHYSICAL SCIENCE

For all its importance, a water molecule is remarkably simple in design: three atoms—two hydrogen (H) and one oxygen (O)—which is why you might have heard it referred to as "H_2O." The chemical bonds in water give it its cohesive quality, meaning that it sticks together. This is why water has a skin-like surface that insects like water striders can float on (as can objects such as paper clips—try it!). It's also why water does not come apart when trees suck it all the way up from their roots to their leaves.

Water is the only substance that occurs naturally as a liquid at Earth's normal temperature. It's also the only one that can take the form of a solid, liquid, or gas. The ability to move between these three forms within the narrow range of Earth's temperatures and pressures means that water is continually passing through the hydrologic cycle: evaporating from bodies of water as vapor, forming into clouds (a process called *condensation*), and falling again as precipitation, either rain or snow. This cycle supplies freshwater to all the Earth's animals and plants and transports nutrients to aquatic ecosystems.

EDUCATIONAL VIDEO

THE GREAT AQUA ADVENTURE

Check out this video about the water cycle.

The hydrologic cycle has a direct influence on our weather and climate. As the sun warms the ocean and causes water to evaporate, heat is stored in the vapor. When the vapor cools into clouds, this heat is released into the air. This cycle helps move heat from the ocean's surface into the atmosphere and eventually around the globe. Ocean currents distribute heat, too. From the equator, where the sun's rays hit Earth most directly, currents move warm

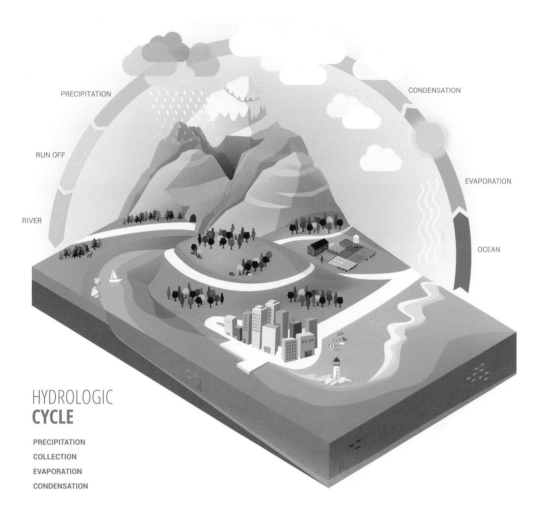

HYDROLOGIC
CYCLE

PRECIPITATION
COLLECTION
EVAPORATION
CONDENSATION

The water cycle in nature.

water outward toward the North and South Poles, then bring cool water back to the equator. Without this continual movement, the Earth's temperatures would be much more extreme.

Water is often referred to as the "universal **solvent**" for its ability to dissolve almost any substance. This is vital to all life on Earth, since the chemical reactions that keep life going must take place in a liquid. Water dissolves molecules so they can react with each other. It also transports essential substances, including nutrients, chemicals, and metabolites, within cells, bodies, and throughout the planet.

WE'RE ALL WATER

John Lennon and Yoko Ono once recorded a song called "We're All Water." They weren't too far off. The average adult male is 60 percent water, and the average

Perspiration is the body's way of cooling someone down during periods of exertion or intense heat.

▼▼▼▼▼▼▼▼▼▼▼▼▼▼▼▼▼▼▼▼▼▼▼▼▼▼▼▼▼▼▼▼▼▼▼

WHAT'S THE SOLUTION?

So why is water so good at dissolving so many types of substances? The answer lies in its structure: the hydrogen and oxygen atoms of water each have different charges. Positively charged hydrogen atoms pull to one side of the molecule, while negatively charged oxygen atoms pull to the other. This polarity, or state of having two opposing charges, allows water molecules to attract a variety of other molecules. For instance, when sodium chloride (commonly referred to as table salt) is added to water, the positive hydrogen atoms attract the negative chloride atoms and the negative oxygen atoms attract the positive sodium atoms. This causes the salt to dissolve.

▲▲▲▲▲▲▲▲▲▲▲▲▲▲▲▲▲▲▲▲▲▲▲▲▲▲▲▲▲▲▲▲▲▲

female is not far behind at 55 percent. Water has many functions throughout the human body, from regulating temperature to flushing out toxins and other harmful waste products to lubricating the motion of the joints. It's not just to slake our thirst—water is essential for our very survival.

Because so much of our body is made up of water, and because water stores heat well and does not rapidly swing from hot to cold, it naturally regulates our body temperature. Water also cools us: when the temperature outside rises above our internal temperature, such as when we're exercising vigorously, glands in the body release sweat through the pores in our skin. This is called perspiring. Sweat is mostly water, and when it evaporates off the surface of the skin, it cools the body down.

Water keeps all the tissues of the body moist, and it keeps the eyes, mouth, nose, and throat from drying out. Significant dryness can lead to inflammation of the tissues, pain, and other complications. A clear fluid called *cerebrospinal fluid* (CSF) cushions the brain and spinal cord and protects them against shock.

CSF is 99 percent water. Water also surrounds the joins so they can move freely and easily, and it helps remove waste products like acidic crystals that can build up in the joints.

We also need plenty of water for proper digestion. Water produces the saliva necessary to break down food. The kidneys, liver, and intestines use water to remove toxins from the system and eliminate them from the body through urination and defecation. Water can prevent constipation by softening stools so they are easier to pass. Besides getting rid of toxins, water breaks down vital nutrients like proteins and carbohydrates so the body can absorb and use them. Without water to shuttle these nutrients throughout the body, we would not be able to perform the most basic functions like breathing or muscle contraction.

HEALTH BENEFITS

The functions and health benefits of water seem endless. Blood, for instance, is 82 percent water—and without blood carrying oxygen to all the cells of your body, they would not be able to work. Water is also the main carrier of electrolytes. An electrolyte is a mineral that acquires an electric charge when dissolved in water; some common examples include sodium, potassium, and calcium. Electrolytes are critical for many of the body's processes, like sending the electric signals that keep the heart pumping and the nerves signaling. Bodily fluids like urine, blood, and sweat all contain electrolytes. Since the body periodically loses some of these fluids, it is necessary to replenish our water supply so we can keep our electrolyte levels balanced.

Water benefits other organs, too, like our skin and kidneys. The effect of proper hydration on the skin has been debated, but, like the other organs in the body, the skin is made of cells and therefore needs water to stay oxygenated, free of toxins, and supplied with nutrients. Skin that is dehydrated, or lacking adequate water, can become dry and flaky, and it is more prone to cracking and irritation. Beware

It's important to stay hydrated when exercising.

of claims about water as a magic cure-all for acne, though. Water will go to other organs before it reaches the skin, and it doesn't supply enough moisture alone to open up pores and allow them to drain.

The kidneys remove waste products from our bloodstream, help keep our fluids in balance, and process waste and extra water into urine. This is why they're sometimes called the body's "trash collectors." Drinking enough water ensures the kidneys can flush waste out of the body and that the blood can transport vital nutrients to them so they can work properly.

Kidney stones are clumps of minerals and other substances that have crystallized in the kidneys. There is no definitive proof that drinking water will prevent the

LIFE ON MARS?

There's a reason why astronomers say to "follow the water" in their search for life on other planets: where there is water, there's a chance that it's acting as a solvent to break down and create new (possibly living) substances. After landing on Mars in 2012, NASA's rover *Curiosity*—an automated vehicle that records data and images of the planet—located an ancient streambed that could have supported life. In 2015, NASA scientists used telescopes to estimate the amount of water that once covered the surface of Mars. They determined that over 4 billion years ago, an ocean larger than Earth's Arctic Ocean occupied half of the planet's northern hemisphere. In some places it could have been over a mile deep. Some of this water is still on Mars, trapped under ice caps and below the ground, but about 87 percent of it has been lost to space.

A photo of Mount Sharp, taken on Mars by the Curiosity *rover in 2012.*

formation of kidney stones, but having plenty of fluids circulating through the kidneys does make it less likely for minerals to stick together. Water may also help prevent urinary tract infections (UTIs), which are caused by bacteria in the urinary tract. Water helps clear the bacteria away before it can cause an infection.

TEXT-DEPENDENT QUESTIONS

1. What are the atoms that make up a molecule of water?
2. What is one way that water can cool us?
3. Describe the function of the kidneys, and how water can help them stay healthy.

RESEARCH PROJECT

Select a body of water on Earth—it could be a river, lake, ocean, or even a small brook in your town. Research the geological history, size, and depth of this body of water, as well as how humans have used it throughout the centuries. Look for current information on environmental challenges the body of water is facing, too, such as pollution or overfishing, and what is being done to solve these problems. Write a brief report summarizing your findings.

CHAPTER

2

STAYING HYDRATED

WORDS TO UNDERSTAND

amino acids: organic molecules that combine to form proteins.

dehydration: losing more water from the body than can be adequately replenished.

dilute: to make something weaker by the addition of water.

hyponatremia: a condition caused by consuming too much fluid, resulting in dangerously low sodium levels in the blood.

overhydration: a condition caused by drinking too much water; it can lead to electrolyte imbalance, low sodium levels, and other issues.

The importance of water can't be underestimated. A human being can go about three weeks without eating, but no more than a week without drinking water. The time frame could be even shorter in harsher conditions, such as extreme heat or coupled with periods of intense exercise. We lose water with every drop of sweat and trip to the bathroom, and we even lose it when we breathe: the air we exhale contains water vapor, which you can see condensing on a cold day. Sicknesses that involve diarrhea, fever, and vomiting can also force a person to lose water quickly. According to a 2012 study at the University of Connecticut, even mild levels of dehydration—defined as 1.5 percent loss of normal water level in the body—can have an effect on a person's mood, energy level, and ability to focus.

Although "eight by eight" is easy to remember, it does not have to be taken literally.

ON THE LEVEL

Whether you're sweating profusely in a hot climate or sitting in an air-conditioned classroom, dehydration can affect you. One key to avoiding it is to parcel out your fluid intake throughout the day. Exactly how much water a person needs depends on factors like climate (we lose lots of water through sweat on hotter days), activity level (vigorous exercise requires more water for the body to function properly), and health (people with medical conditions like diabetes or heart disease, or who take medications that can cause them to urinate excessively, need to watch their water intake carefully). For younger people, some basic recommendations for daily water intake are:

- *4–8 years*: 5 eight-ounce cups per day
- *9–13 years*: 7–8 eight-ounce cups per day
- *14–18 years*: 8–11 eight-ounce cups per day

This may sound like a lot of water, but keep in mind that these recommendations are for total intake, meaning they include water that's part of other beverages and food. (Find more on food as a source of water below.) According to the Institute of Medicine, an adequate intake for adult men is about 13 cups (3 liters), and 9 cups (2.2 liters) for

WARNING SIGNS

Besides thirst, the body comes equipped with other warnings signs to let us know if we're getting dehydrated. A dry mouth from a lack of saliva is one. This can also cause bad breath, since saliva helps control bacteria growth in the mouth; not having enough means that foul-smelling bacteria can multiply more easily. Other symptoms include:

- *Cool or dry skin.* When our bodies are low on water, they may tap fluids in the skin, resulting in coolness or dryness.
- *Fatigue, dizziness, or headache.* These symptoms are tied to the fact that so much of our blood is made up of water; the less water in our systems, the lower our blood volume, which can lead to feelings of dizziness and disorientation.
- *Lack of urine.* This is an important one. If your urine is especially dark (the color of apple juice or darker) or especially pungent, or if you stop urinating for 12 hours or longer, you could be at risk for dehydration. Urine that is clear or pale yellow in color indicate that water levels are good.

women. Another rule of thumb, especially for adults, is to divide body weight by two and drink that amount of water in ounces. For instance, a 180-pound man would want to ingest 90 ounces of water (about 11 cups) each day.

For years, a common way to remember how much water to drink has been the "eight-by-eight" rule: drink eight 8-ounce glasses per day, and you should meet your needs. This rule has its origins in a 1945 U.S. government recommendation that people get 2.5 liters of water per day, about the equivalent of eight glasses. However, the recommendation also stated that a good percentage of this water can come from prepared foods. The "eight-by-eight" rule has stuck around because it's so easy to remember, but it doesn't need to be taken literally: the equivalent of eight glasses of fluid from a variety of sources should be sufficient for most people.

HYDRATING FOODS AND OTHER BEVERAGES

In addition to water, many foods and other beverages can provide hydration. According to the Institute of Medicine, about 20 percent of a person's fluid intake comes from food sources. Some fruits and vegetables are over 90 percent water, making them good choices to replenish fluids *and* provide much-needed natural sugars, electrolytes, vitamins, minerals, and amino acids. Some hydrating fruits and vegetables to reach for include:

- **Watermelon.** Fitting for its name, a slice of watermelon is a whopping 92 percent water. It also has essential calcium and magnesium that boost the body's ability to rehydrate.
- **Cucumbers.** These contain even more water by percentage than watermelons, at 96 percent. They also have lots of vitamin K, which helps with blood clotting. Try mashing some cucumber slices into a glass of water to add flavor and nutrients.
- **Iceberg lettuce.** While this one isn't known for its nutritional profile, it does contain 96 percent water. Spinach is a more nutrient-rich option and, at 92 percent water, can still help you rehydrate. Eggplant, tomatoes, broccoli, and cantaloupe are other high-water food options.

When it comes to beverages, milk is a top choice for rehydration. One 2011 study showed that it is even better than sports drinks or water after a workout because of its protein, calcium, and carbohydrates. Since the fat in whole milk can interfere with fluid absorption, fat-free or skim varieties are preferable. Coconut water has a unique, nutty taste and can be hydrating. It is high in potassium but lacks sodium, something we need to replenish after sweating. Soda can be a way to hydrate, too, but it's high in sugar and caffeine. Caffeine doesn't dehydrate you, but it can increase urine output for the first few hours after drinking.

Sports drinks provide electrolytes like sodium and potassium and energy-producing carbohydrates. However, they also contain a lot of sugar—sometimes as much as 10 teaspoons per serving—and unnecessary calories. If you're an endurance athlete or working out for over an hour at a time, sports drinks can be an alternative to water. But for most people, plain old water is the safest, healthiest way to hydrate.

Watermelon got its name from its high water content.

Although sports drinks are advertised as perfect for rehydration, they often contain additives that you may be better off without.

Special Concerns for Athletes

Speaking of athletes, they need to pay special attention to their water intake. They sweat more, for one thing. A high school football player wearing pads and a helmet may lose as much as five pounds in sweat during a rigorous summer practice. If this liquid isn't replaced, fluid levels drop and perspiration—the body's main cooling mechanism—can stop, causing body temperatures to rise to dangerously high levels.

Adequate water intake can also make workouts more efficient. Dehydration lowers blood volume, meaning the heart has to pump harder and faster. Having enough water means the heart isn't as strained. Water facilitates the transport of nutrients and oxygen, both essential for athletic activity.

Some sports medicine professionals advocate hydrating before you hit the track, trail, or gym. Fifteen to 20 ounces of water 1 to 2 hours before exercise and another 8 to 10 ounces 15 minutes before are standard recommendations. Periodic water breaks—about 8 ounces every 15 minutes—help put back in all you're sweating out.

A word of caution, though: there are dangers to overhydration, or drinking too much water, during athletic events. In rare cases, overhydration can lead to a dangerous condition called hyponatremia. This is when a person consumes so much fluid that he or she can't get rid of the excess by sweating or urinating. High water levels dilute the blood and cause sodium levels to fall. The body pulls water from the blood into nearby cells to balance sodium levels, and the cells start to swell. In some cases, this can be deadly.

The best gauge for how much to drink is your thirst. Drink up when you're thirsty, but don't chug a huge amount of fluid all at once. If you aren't feeling well during a workout, stop exercising and take a rest in a cool spot to lower your core temperature.

EDUCATIONAL VIDEO

WHAT IF YOU STOPPED DRINKING WATER?

Check out this video about the importance of water to the human body.

DEHYDRATION DOUBTERS

Make no mistake: getting enough water in the system is one of the first rules of health. But there are some scientists, sports nutritionists, and other health-care professionals who believe the threat of dehydration is overstated. They point to the fact that some hydration studies, such as one in 2012 that declared two-thirds of children in New York and Los Angeles weren't getting enough water, have been funded by bottled water and

HYDRATION STATIONS

There may be some scientific back-and-forth about water's health benefits and how widespread a problem dehydration is, but keeping tabs on your water intake is never a bad idea. Some people find the taste of water bland, or they don't remember to drink water in the middle of a busy day. Here are some tips for spicing up your water and staying hydrated on the go:

- *Flavor plain water.* By adding fruit or a splash of juice, you can improve the taste of water so you'll crave it more.

- *Pack a bottle.* Having a bottle with you makes it easy to sip water throughout the day. When it's super hot in the summer, try freezing the bottle the night before. By midday the ice will have melted, making for a cool and refreshing thirst quencher.

- *Swap out snacks.* Replacing a midday snack of chips or pretzels a few days a week with fruit or raw vegetables can help boost hydration levels.

It's never a bad idea to have a bottle of water along for the ride.

sports drink companies. This "industry science" presents a conflict of interests and may lead to trumped-up claims about people's hydration needs.

Skeptics also point to the lack of medical evidence for water being a magical cure for everything from depression to headaches, or a way to lose weight or improve organ function. Chronic dehydration may increase the likelihood of kidney stones, but a bout of mild dehydration, they argue, is not the end of the world. Skeptics also say that certain ways we measure dehydration are inherently flawed. For instance, studies have used a particular level of urine concentration in children as a mark of dehydration, when in fact, that level is fairly average.

Whatever the case, drinking water is still a good habit. While it won't solve every health problem, it can help the body run more smoothly and efficiently. Everyone's hydration needs are different, depending on what they eat, what sort of climate they live in, and other factors. By monitoring your thirst—especially in hot or dry environments, or during periods of intense exercise—and eating a range of fruits and vegetables in addition to taking fluids, you should go a long way in staying properly hydrated.

Text-Dependent Questions

1. Does every person need the exact same amount of water?
2. Name two foods that have high water content.
3. Can you drink too much water? If so, what are some related health issues?

Research Project

Research a place in the world where chronic dehydration is a problem. Try to find out the causes of water shortage or poor water quality, the effects dehydration is having on the population, and what solutions are being proposed, including new technologies. Write a brief report summarizing your findings.

IMPORTANCE AND SCARCITY

 ## WORDS TO UNDERSTAND

aquifer: an underground layer of rock that can contain and move water.

corrosion: the process of wearing down or damaging something, such as stone or metals, by chemical action over time.

ethanol: an alcohol made from plant materials, sometimes used as a fuel source.

genetic modification: the practice of modifying the DNA of a living organism in order to obtain a desired characteristic.

infrastructure: the basic framework necessary for a society to function, including roads, buildings, and water and power utilities.

irrigation: the process of directing water to crops.

runoff: water that is not absorbed by the ground and drains off the surface of land, often carrying pollutants or other materials.

subsidy: money given by the government to help industries and businesses stay competitive.

I t's one thing to make sure that we as individuals drink enough water on a day-to-day basis. It's another challenge altogether to make sure that we have the infrastructure necessary to transport this water from reservoirs, rivers, and other sources to our homes, schools, and businesses. Events in the city of Flint, Michigan, in the early 2010s illustrate both the importance of safe drinking water and the many pitfalls that can interrupt its delivery.

THE FLINT WATER CRISIS

In 2011, the city of Flint was facing a budget crisis. Many of the auto-manufacturing plants that once provided jobs to residents had left the area, destroying what's known as the "tax base," meaning the amount of money that the government can collect in taxes and use to provide services. The state of Michigan took over the city's budget and immediately looked for ways to save money. One of the cost-cutting measures proposed was to switch the city's water supply from the more expensive Detroit system, which used water from Lake Huron, to the Flint River. A study found that the river water would be undrinkable unless it was treated with a special anti-corrosion additive. Without the additive, the water could eat away at the pipes of the delivery system and release harmful lead and bacteria into the water supply.

Despite these warnings, local officials went ahead and used the Flint River supply anyway, without treating it first. The switch took place in April 2014. By May, Flint residents were complaining about the color, taste, and odor of the water coming into their homes. Bacteria was detected in the water in August. Officials added more chlorine to the water and advised residents to boil it as a safety precaution. In October, the nearby General Motors auto plant stopped using the water because it was corroding car parts.

The following year, tests revealed high levels of lead in the water of many Flint-area homes. Exposure to lead can have many dire health consequences, including stunted growth, damage to the brain and nervous system, and increased risk of miscarriage. Local officials disputed the tests, but the problem did not go away. In September 2015, a group of doctors found that lead levels in some local children had doubled or even tripled. Again, officials claimed the water was OK and blamed seasonal changes for the rise in lead levels. But when government scientists confirmed the doctors' findings, the

National Guardsmen distributed bottled water to citizens of Flint in 2016, two years into the water crisis.

governor of Michigan, Rick Snyder, was finally forced to take action. He distributed water filters, ordered water testing in schools, and announced plans to reconnect Flint to the safer Detroit water supply in October 2015.

But the problem was far from over. Lead levels remained high as Flint transitioned to the Detroit supply, because the Flint water had corroded the iron and lead pipes that delivered the water to people's homes. The city declared a state of emergency in December 2015, and state and national emergencies were declared in January 2016. The federal government began providing equipment and resources, and the state government said it would finally begin replacing Flint's 8,000 lead water pipes. But such massive structural improvements take time; even in 2017, Flint residents were still being advised to boil water before using it for drinking or cooking.

LAWN MAINTENANCE

Of the over 300 gallons (1,135.6 liters) of water the average American family uses each day, about a third of it goes to landscaping, watering lawns and gardens, and other outdoor uses. Front lawns may spruce up a property (and are something of an American tradition), but they can drink up a lot of precious water. This is especially true in dry areas such as the American Southwest, where many grasses used for lawns are not native to the region and require extra water. Organizations such as the Environmental Protection Agency (EPA) recommend using native grass species instead, since they can grow with the region's natural rainfall.

Maintaining green lawns can require a lot of water.

Some fresh water is trapped in glaciers, such as the Perito Moreno Glacier in Argentina.

LIMITED ACCESS

There are many lessons to take away from the Flint water crisis: including the need for improved infrastructure, the importance of administrative oversight, and the dangers of ignoring warning signs—to name just a few. But perhaps the biggest lesson is one that impacts all of us: the value of clean drinking water, and just how scarce it can be.

CALIFORNIA CRISIS

 Between 2011 and 2014, the state of California experienced one of the worst droughts in its history. As the drought carried over into 2015, Governor Jerry Brown ordered mandatory restrictions on water consumption that aimed to reduce the state's overall use by 25 percent. The restrictions were lifted in 2016 after drought conditions moderately improved. Some of the conservation measures were made permanent, including prohibitions on watering street medians, watering lawns up to 48 hours after a rainfall, and washing cars without a hose fitted with a shut-off nozzle.

Parched farmland near Sacramento, California, at the height of the drought.

We tend to think of water as a widely available, endlessly replenished resource. After all, it covers 70 percent of the planet, right? And it's not as though it *goes* anywhere—rain, snow, and sleet ensure water is continually recycled. The problem is, we humans need freshwater for drinking, farming, cooking, and hygiene, and the majority of the world's supply is salty ocean water. This water is useless to humans (except for swimming, of course) unless the salt is removed—a costly, energy-consuming process. Only 2.5 percent of the world's water is fresh. What's more, only a meager 1 percent is easily accessible; the rest is trapped in glaciers, snowfields, or hard-to-reach underground lakes called aquifers.

There are other problems besides the scarcity of freshwater. One is that freshwater is unevenly distributed: fewer than 10 countries possess 60 percent of the world's available supply. As the global population continues to grow, competition for these limited freshwater resources increases. The effects of climate change, which can alter weather patterns, temperatures, and rainfall cycles around the globe, will only make freshwater availability more unpredictable in the coming years. Add to this the fact that humans have polluted some of these sources, as well as pumped out more freshwater than can be replaced to meet growing demand, and the future of freshwater looks grim indeed. It is estimated that 1.8 billion people will live in water-impoverished areas by 2025.

Water and Agriculture

Humans use water in three major ways: domestically (in their homes), for industry, and for agriculture. Of these, agriculture is by far the most prevalent, accounting for some 70 percent of global freshwater use. The issue of dwindling freshwater resources will only make it harder to feed the world's growing population.

One problem is that many current agricultural methods do not use water very efficiently. Faulty irrigation systems that leak water, cultivating crops that are ill-suited to their environments (such as growing "thirsty" crops like cotton or rice in traditionally dry lands), and unsustainable irrigation methods like "field flooding" (drenching a field with water to let it soak into the soil, resulting in excess **runoff**) all contribute to wasted water.

While this waste is a very real problem, sometimes farmers have no choice. In poorer parts of the world, field flooding may be the only option, since more high-tech, efficient irrigation systems are costly to install. Farmers who need to make short-term profits may grow "thirsty" crops to keep pace with the market. Sometimes, government **subsidies** can encourage water waste: the U.S. government, for instance, has helped subsidize irrigation for decades, taking away the incentive for farmers to conserve water.

Governments can use legislation to affect which crops are grown, too; for example, a 2007 law that required all U.S. gasoline to contain a certain amount of **ethanol**. The measure was intended to help the environment, since ethanol is thought to be more eco-friendly than fossil fuels. But the huge amount of corn it takes to make this ethanol has its own environmental consequences, including water waste and pollution from fertilizers. Many politicians, environmentalists, and scientists have questioned whether these effects from ethanol production are worse than the problems it was designed to avoid.

Watering a wheat field.

WHAT IS TO BE DONE?

Strategies to solve the impending water crisis focus on improving efficiency. This starts by acknowledging that freshwater is a limited resource and that every drop we use in our fields, factories, and homes must be put to good use. Since agriculture takes up so much of our freshwater supply, those in the industry could experiment with irrigation systems such as "drip" lines that feed water directly to the roots of plants. These sorts of systems have already reduced water consumption and improved

EDUCATIONAL VIDEO

ON DROUGHT AND DEFORESTATION

Check out this news report on the 2014 Brazilian Drought.

farm output in dry areas of the Middle East. Farmers can also improve soil structure—the arrangement of soil particles that determines how well the soil binds together—by fertilizing with organic materials such as mulch. This helps lock in moisture and improves the soil's strength and water-retaining properties. Genetic modification, while still a controversial practice, can be used to develop more water-efficient crops.

There have already been strides in industry-related water efficiency. The Intel computer company in Chandler, Arizona, pumps 2 million gallons of wastewater daily to a treatment plant, where it is then purified and sent back into an aquifer to be used by the local population. Organizations such as the Alliance for Water Efficiency recommend that companies look to implement similar water treatment, recycling, and reuse programs within their factories. Even less expensive improvements can go a long way in improving industrial water efficiency, such as using low-volume nozzles on spray washers, repairing all leaks as soon as they are detected, and installing low-flow toilets in factory restrooms.

It's not only large-scale farms and factories that are responsible for conserving our water supply—at the most basic level, each and every individual bears some of the responsibility, too. In our own homes, we can implement many simple practices that can help. For example,

FURTHER SOLUTIONS

Environmentalists and those who study sustainable practices have offered many other possible ideas to trim worldwide water use and ensure we have enough for the years ahead. Here are a few:

- *Construct desalination plants.* Desalination is the process of removing salt from seawater. The practice of boiling seawater to purify it is an ancient one. Today's desalination plants use ultra-fine membranes and high pressure to strain minerals and salts from water. It is an energy-intensive process, though some plants are beginning to use solar power as a "greener" alternative. The largest desalination plant in the Western Hemisphere opened in 2015 in Carlsbad, California.

- *Improve rainwater catchment systems.* Another ancient practice, the collection and storage of rainwater is a good way to maximize water efficiency. In drought-prone countries like India and Pakistan, revamped rainwater catchment systems (such as underground tanks called cisterns) are improving water access in villages and urban areas.

- *Education.* As the freshwater crisis spreads, and periods of drought become a "new normal" for populations worldwide, education and awareness about the seriousness of the problem can help people change their water-consumption habits on an individual and collective level. Until water conservation becomes a learned habit in younger generations, we will continue to face difficulty overcoming the freshwater crisis.

turning off the tap for the minute that you brush your teeth or wash your hands saves over two gallons of water. You can save the water you use to cook pasta, let it cool, and reuse it for watering plants or even as a base for soup stock. Cutting down on shower time and electricity use (since power plants are huge users of water) are some other ways to reduce water waste.

A minor step like turning off the water while you brush your teeth can, over time, add up to a lot of saved water.

TEXT-DEPENDENT QUESTIONS

1. In a few words, describe the cause of the Flint water crisis.
2. Why is freshwater so important, and why is it so rare?
3. Name two sources of agricultural water waste.

RESEARCH PROJECT

Research a country other than the United States that has recently faced (within the past 5 to 10 years) or is currently facing a drought. Some examples include China, Ethiopia, South Africa, and Brazil. Write a brief report detailing the location of the drought within the country, its causes, and its effects on the human population, agriculture, and the environment. Include any plans of the government or international organizations to solve the problem.

BOTTLED UP

Words to Understand

biodegrade: when a substance is broken down naturally by elements in the environment.

carbonated: a substance, such as a beverage, containing carbon dioxide, which gives it a bubbly, fizzy quality.

carcinogen: something that causes cancer.

condense: to change from a gas or vapor into a denser liquid state.

filtration: the process of passing water through membranes that catch contaminants and other solids.

ion: an atom or group of atoms with an electric charge.

municipal: of or relating to a city or town or its local government.

A walk through the average American grocery store, convenience store, or even gas station will provide no evidence that several areas of the world have recently faced (or are currently facing) freshwater droughts. Cases of bottled water line the shelves, their colorful labels adorned with images of natural springs or flowing mountain rivers. The easy access and disposability of bottled water can make us take it for granted; we can guzzle it without having to think about how far it traveled to reach us or where the used bottles go. And it's not only plain bottled water that crowds store shelves: all sorts of special varieties—including mineral, sparkling, flavored, and vitamin-enhanced waters—compete with the regular stuff, too. How do we begin to make sense of all these options—and, more importantly, what are the best water choices for the long-term health of the planet?

Setting the Standards

Every year, $100 billion is spent on bottled water worldwide. The United States alone goes through 50 billion water bottles a year, and water was expected to outpace soda as the most popular American beverage by the end of 2016. This statistic is all the more staggering when you consider that bottled water costs 2,000 times as much as tap water. Yet with problems of water contamination in the news, such as the Flint water crisis, people are willing to pay a premium for what they perceive as a safer alternative. Others just like the taste, or they prefer bottled water for its convenience.

Tap water is regulated by the Environmental Protection Agency (EPA) and must meet standards set by the Safe Drinking Water Act (SDWA), a 1974 law that set maximum levels for different contaminants in drinking water. Bottled water is treated as a food product and does not fall under this act. It is regulated by the Food and Drug Administration (FDA). Proponents of bottled water say that FDA regulations are just as strict as EPA regulations, but detractors point to the fact that bottled water manufacturers do not have to disclose important information about the source, treatment methods, and potential contaminants of their products.

EDUCATIONAL VIDEO

FROM SOURCE TO TAP

Check out a video about how water gets into your taps.

The regulations for bottled water can be quite different from those for tap water. In some cases, FDA regulations for bottled water are more stringent than the EPA's are for tap. For instance, the acceptable limit on lead in tap water is higher than in bottled water, due to the fact that many old households and water systems have lead pipes that have to be accounted for. On the other hand, some EPA regulations are more stringent, rather than less. Tap water is required

Regulations for tap water differ from regulations for bottled water.

WELL WATER

 About 10 percent of the U.S. population relies on private wells for their home water supplies. Wells draw directly from groundwater stored in aquifers. They are popular in rural areas, where homeowners are farther away from the water delivery systems of urban areas. Private wells are not regulated by the EPA, so homeowners are responsible for testing, maintaining, and protecting the safety of their well water. Common pollutants in well water include chemicals from fertilizers and pesticides, especially in agricultural areas. Well users should test their water a minimum of once a year.

An old-fashioned pump for an underground well.

to be tested more often for bacteria than bottled water. In 2015, 14 brands of bottled water had to be recalled for possible exposure to the harmful *E. coli* bacteria. Water that is bottled and sold within the same state does not require FDA regulation; this task is given over to the individual states, which means that standards can vary from place to place. The International Bottled Water Association (IBWA) administers a separate set of standards for its members.

Types of Bottled Water

The FDA recognizes several major types of bottled waters. Most bottled water is classified as "spring water." This means that it comes from an underground source, or spring, and rises to the surface on its own. It is either gathered from the surface of the spring or collected through a hole drilled underground. Beware of terms like "mountain water" or "100 percent pure" to advertise spring water, as these are not regulated by the FDA. Also, some spring waters are not bottled at the source, but trucked back to separate bottling facilities. During the course of transit, additives like chlorine may be put in the water that are then removed prior to bottling.

Purified water may come from the same source as spring water or from a public supply. Most spring water undergoes some type of filtration, but purified water is subjected to additional treatment processes to reduce impurities to very low levels. These processes include:

- **Distillation.** Here, the water is boiled into a vapor that is collected in a clean container. Minerals and solid contaminants do not vaporize, so when the vapor is cooled and condenses, only purified water is left behind.
- **Deionization.** In this process, special substances are used to attract mineral ions in water, which are then replaced with water ions. This removes solids from the water and leaves it in a more purified state.
- **Reverse osmosis.** This is a kind of intensified filtration process in which pressurized water is forced through an ultrafine membrane that screens out ions, molecules, and other contaminants.

Other types of bottled water recognized by the FDA include *artesian* water, *mineral* water, and *sparkling* water. Artesian water comes from a confined aquifer. The pressure of the aquifer forces the water upward, where it is drawn out of the earth by a well. According to the FDA definition, the water drawn must already be sitting above the uppermost level of the aquifer. The name *artesian* comes from the Roman city of Artesium, where many of these wells were drilled in the Middle Ages.

Mineral water is similar to spring water in that it comes from an underground source, only it must contain at least 250 parts per million of dissolved solids. These are minerals and trace elements such as calcium and potassium. "Parts per million" is a way of describing how much of one substance is contained within another. To say "250 parts per million" means that there are 250 parts of dissolved solids for every million parts of water. If you picture a giant gumball machine holding a million gumballs as a representation of a mineral water sample, at least 250 of those gumballs would have to represent dissolved solids. According to the FDA, dissolved solids must be present at the water source and not added afterwards.

Finally, sparkling water is recognizable for its bubbly, fizzy quality. Sometimes it's referred to as "carbonated water" because it contains dissolved carbon dioxide, which gives it its bubbles. Natural sparkling water has this carbonation present at its source, whether it's a spring or artesian well. The FDA allows carbon dioxide to be removed during processing, but it must be replaced to the original level found at the source before being bottled and sold. Mineral water can also be natural sparkling water.

Environmental Ethics

There is no doubt that bottled water has an impact on the environment. Most water bottles are made of a special plastic known as polyethylene terephthalate (PET). PET is recyclable, though only about 31 percent ever gets recycled; the rest ends up in landfills, incinerators (where it is burned, releasing harmful pollutants in the process), or is just tossed aside as litter.

What's more, PET does not biodegrade the way organic matter such as food scraps and grass clippings do. Instead, it is broken down into tiny pieces by the sun in a process known as *photodegradation*. It can take a bottle a long time—perhaps many centuries—to break down in this way. Unlike biodegradable materials, these tiny plastic pieces do not harmlessly re-enter soil, water, or other living systems; they continue to exist untransformed as plastic, and can have a toxic effect on their surroundings. Bottles that make their way out to the ocean can have devastating effects on marine life. Plastic particles pollute the water and poison fish and other marine animals. Animals further up the food chain—including us— can end up ingesting these toxic particles if we consume affected fish.

It isn't just getting rid of the packaging that's a problem. Producing water bottles takes up a lot of energy—about 17 million barrels of oil during the year 2006 alone, according to the Pacific Institute. And that doesn't include all the fossil fuels necessary to pump, treat, package, cool, and ship bottled water around the country. Ironically, it also takes water to make water: when you calculate all the processes that go into making the bottles, printing the labels, and other production details, it takes about 1.63 liters of water to make 1 liter of sellable bottled water. Add to all of this the amount of carbon dioxide released into the atmosphere through production, transport, and plastic incineration, and it becomes clear that tap water is the "greener" option.

Besides the environmental impact, there is a less-often discussed issue with bottled water: the slow privatization of what has long been held as a public good. The more water people buy in bottles, the less likely they are to care about the health and upkeep of their public water systems. This creates a divide between those rich enough to purchase their own water supply and those who still rely on public infrastructure. As we've seen in Flint, the safety of that infrastructure is already being threatened by age and lack of

Plastic bottles at a recycling plant.

WRITTEN IN WATER

The life-giving properties of water have seized the imaginations of poets, mystics, scientists, and ecologists from all eras. Observation of water and meditation on its importance have inspired many memorable quotations. Here is a sampling:

- "Water is the driving force of all nature."—Leonardo da Vinci
- "Nothing is softer or more flexible than water, yet nothing can resist it." —Lao Tzu
- "We forget that the water cycle and the life cycle are one."—Jacques Cousteau
- "The tree that is beside the running water is fresher and gives more fruit." —St. Theresa of Avila
- "No water, no life. No blue, no green."—Sylvia Earle

Source: BrainyQuotes.com.

maintenance. If private water purchasers continue to direct their money to bottled water companies instead of the public supply, the result may well be fewer people having access to good-quality water.

FILTERING THE EVIDENCE

Of course, there are times when bottled water is necessary. In places where people lack access to clean drinking water, where public water systems are in violation of the SDWA, or during emergencies or natural disasters when public works systems are severely compromised, bottled water is a critical backup.

It should also be said that tap water isn't necessarily perfect, either. One study by the Environmental Working Group conducted between 2004 and 2009 found more than 200 unregulated chemicals in the tap water of 45 states. These chemicals came from various sources, including agricultural and urban runoff, wastewater from factories and water treatment facilities, and household items.

But the question of whether bottled water is ultimately any safer is still up for debate. Most evidence points to the fact that bottled water isn't any purer or cleaner than tap water—and, in some cases, it may have more contaminants. In fact, almost half of all bottled water comes from municipal water sources—the same place you get your tap water. (It should be noted that most municipal bottled water receives additional filtration before being resold.) Most tap water is treated with chlorine to prevent the spread of bacteria, while bottled water has no such disinfecting additives. However, a 2012 study estimated that 1.1 million cases of stomach illness each year are due to tainted pipes in water-delivery systems.

There is also the issue of the chemicals within plastic water bottles themselves. Industry professionals insist that PET plastic bottles do not contain the harmful compound bisphenol A (BPA) or chemical phthalates (each linked to health issues, including breast cancer, hormone imbalance, and developmental disorders). Others say that the bottles are safe if they are used only once; if used repeatedly, they can leach harmful chemicals such as DEHA (a possible carcinogen) into the water.

One stage of the water filtration process at a water treatment plant.

With all this conflicting evidence, those who are concerned about the quality of their tap water but also have reservations about the bottled water industry are advised to filter their water at home. There are several types of home water filters, ranging from pitchers with replaceable filter cartridges, to those that mount directly to faucets, to more expensive reverse-osmosis filters that can purify an entire home's water supply. Before purchasing a filter, it is a good idea to test the water coming out of the tap to see what contaminants there are, or at least check your water supplier's "Consumer Confidence Report" through the EPA website for vital information. Otherwise, the filter you purchase may be useless to remove the contaminants that are actually in your water—or, more optimistically, you may find that you do not have to filter at all.

TEXT-DEPENDENT QUESTIONS

1. Are tap water and bottled water regulated by the same organization?
2. Name and describe one method used to make purified water.
3. What are some environmental-related arguments against the use of bottled water?

RESEARCH PROJECT

Find out if the water in your house comes from a private well or public municipal supply. If it comes from a private well, research how the well works and any potential issues you and your family may have to watch out for. If it comes from a municipal supply, research the source of your water, where your wastewater goes, and any recent or current issues your region may be facing with its drinking water supply. You may also try to obtain a copy of the Consumer Confidence Report for the drinking water in your area from the EPA website (www.epa.gov/ccr). Write a brief report summarizing your findings.

FURTHER READING

Books and Articles

Carey, Benedict. "Hard to Swallow." *Los Angeles Times*, November 20, 2000. http://articles.latimes.com/2000/nov/20/health/he-54596.

Glennon, Robert. *Water Follies: Groundwater Pumping and the Fate of America's Fresh Waters*. Washington, DC: Island Press, 2002.

Goodman, Sarah. "Fewer Regulations for Bottled Water Than Tap, GAO Says." *New York Times*, July 9, 2009. http://www.nytimes.com/gwire/2009/07/09/09greenwire-fewer-regulations-for-bottled-water-than-tap-g-33331.html.

Ingram, B. Lynn, and Frances Malamud-Roam. *The West without Water: What Past Floods, Droughts, and Other Climatic Clues Tell Us about Tomorrow*. Berkeley, CA: University of California Press, 2013.

Lund, Jay. "The Coming California Drought in 2017." *KQED Science*, December 2, 2016. https://ww2.kqed.org/science/2016/12/02/the-coming-california-drought-in-2017/.

Newcomber, Laura. "Water Costs Us 2,000 Times More Than Tap. Is It Worth It?" *The Daily Beast*, September 18, 2016. http://www.thedailybeast.com/articles/2016/09/18/bottled-water-costs-us-2-000-times-more-than-tap-is-it-worth-it.html.

Royte, Elizabeth. *Bottlemania: Big Business, Local Springs, and the Battle over America's Drinking Water*. New York: Bloomsbury, 2009.

Schwartz, Judith D. *Water in Plain Sight: Hope for a Thirsty World*. New York: St. Martin's Press, 2016.

Websites

U.S. Geological Survey (USGS): Water Resources of the United States

www2.usgs.gov/water

The USGS maintains an expansive website with all sorts of information about the water resources of the United States.

UN Water

http://www.unwater.org

This website administered by the United Nations has a global focus, covering freshwater management, sanitation, and development projects worldwide.

Scientific American

https://www.scientificamerican.com

The online version of *Scientific American* magazine has many features relating to water, environment, and sustainability, as well as up-to-date science-related news stories.

EDUCATIONAL VIDEOS

Chapter One: Crash Course Kids. "The Great Aqua Adventure: Crash Course Kids #24.1." https://www.youtube.com/watch?v=z5G4NCwWUxY.

Chapter Two: AsapSCIENCE. "What If You Stopped Drinking Water?" https://www.youtube.com/watch?v=zCheAcpFkL8.

Chapter Three: BBC News. "Brazil Drought Linked to Amazon Deforestation." https://www.youtube.com/watch?v=6rQmG-koEPI.

Chapter Four: greentreks. "Clean Water: A Long Journey from the Source to Our Tap." https://www.youtube.com/watch?v=-bvZCdMecEo.

SERIES GLOSSARY

amino acid: an organic molecule that is the building block of proteins.

antibody: a protein in the blood that fights off substances the body thinks are dangerous.

antioxidant: a substance that fights against free radicals, molecules in the body that can damage other cells.

biofortification: the process of improving the nutritional value of crops through breeding or genetic modification.

calories: units of energy.

caramelization: the process by which the natural sugars in foods brown when heated, creating a nutty flavor.

carbohydrates: starches, sugars, and fibers found in food; a main source of energy for the body.

carcinogen: something that causes cancer.

carnivorous: meat-eating.

cholesterol: a soft, waxy substance present in all parts of the body, including the skin, muscles, liver, and intestines.

collagen: a fibrous protein that makes up much of the body's connective tissues.

deficiency: a lack of something, such as a nutrient in one's diet.

derivative: a product that is made from another source; for example, malt comes from barley, making it a barley derivative.

diabetes: a disease in which the body's ability to produce the hormone insulin is impaired.

emulsifiers: chemicals that allow mixtures to blend.

enzyme: a protein that starts or accelerates an action or process within the body.

food additive: a product added to a food to improve flavor, appearance, nutritional value, or shelf life.

genetically modified organism (GMO): a plant or animal that has had its genetic material altered to create new characteristics.

growth hormone: a substance either naturally produced by the body or synthetically made that stimulates growth in animals or plants.

herbicide: a substance designed to kill unwanted plants, such as weeds.

ionizing radiation: a form of radiation that is used in agriculture; foods are exposed to X-rays or other sources of radiation to eliminate microorganisms and insects and make foods safer.

legume: a plant belonging to the pea family, with fruits or seeds that grow in pods.

macronutrients: nutrients required in large amounts for the health of living organisms, including proteins, fats, and carbohydrates.

malnutrition: a lack of nutrients in the diet, due to food inaccessibility, not consuming enough vitamins and minerals, and other factors.

marketing: the way companies advertise their products to consumers.

metabolism: the chemical process by which living cells produce energy.

micronutrients: nutrients required in very small amounts for the health of living organisms.

monoculture farming: the agricultural practice of growing a massive amount of a single crop, instead of smaller amounts of diverse crops.

nutritional profile: the nutritional makeup of given foods, including the balance of vitamins, minerals, proteins, fats, and other components.

obesity: a condition in which excess body fat has amassed to the point where it causes ill-health effects.

pasteurization: a process that kills microorganisms, making certain foods and drinks safer to consume.

pesticide: a substance designed to kill insects or other organisms that can cause damage to plants or animals.

processed food: food that has been refined before resale, often with additional fats, sugars, sodium, and other additives.

protein complementation: the dietary practice of combining different plant-based foods to get all of the essential amino acids.

refined: when referring to grains or flours, describing those that have been processed to remove elements of the whole grain.

savory: a spicy or salty quality in food.

subsidy: money given by the government to help industries and businesses stay competitive.

sustainable: a practice that can be successfully maintained over a long period of time.

vegan: a person who does not eat meat, poultry, fish, dairy, or other products sourced from animals.

vegetarian: a person who does not eat meat, poultry, or fish.

whole grain: grains that have been minimally processed and contain all three main parts of the grain—the bran, the germ, and the endosperm.

INDEX

ABOUT THE AUTHOR

Michael Centore is a writer and editor. He has helped produce many titles, including memoirs, cookbooks, and educational materials, for a variety of publishers. He has authored numerous books for Mason Crest, including titles in the Major Nations in a Global World and Drug Addiction and Recovery series. His work has appeared in the *Los Angeles Review of Books, Killing the Buddha, Mockingbird,* and other print- and web-based publications. He lives in Connecticut.

PHOTO CREDITS